**DATE DUE**   APR 0 5

| | | | |
|---|---|---|---|
| | | | |
| | | | |
| | | | |
| | | | |
| | | | |
| | | | |
| | | | |
| | | | |
| | | | |
| | | | |
| | | | |
| | | | |
| | | | |
| | | | |
| | | | |
| | | | |
| GAYLORD | | | PRINTED IN U.S.A. |

# GO FLY A BIKE!

# Go Fly a Bike!

• THE ULTIMATE BOOK ABOUT BICYCLE FUN, FREEDOM & SCIENCE •

by **Bill Haduch**

illustrated by **Chris Murphy**

# DUTTON CHILDREN'S BOOKS • New York

CIP Data is available.

Published in the United States by Dutton Children's Books,
a division of Penguin Young Readers Group
345 Hudson Street, New York, New York 10014
www.penguin.com
Designed by Richard Amari
Printed in USA • First Edition
ISBN 0-525-47024-7
2 4 6 8 10 9 7 5 3 1

To Dad, his red Ross cruiser,
and his ride to the Forty Fort Airport

B.H.

## ACKNOWLEDGMENTS

Paula and Jim Grill, Vince Menci, Nick Engler, Robert Petersen, Jess Brallier, Wesley Posvar, Sheldon Brown, the Tunkhannok crew, the Delaware Water Gap crew, the dolphin trainer who saved me in the Keys, Henry Ihling, Walter Gorecki, Cecilia Posluzny, Greg LeMond, Marty Nothstein, and Ashley Kimmet

# contents

# GO FLY A BIKE!

*Pssst!* Wanna flip? Use your thumb to quickly zip through these pages like a flip book. See if you can make this kid and his woofie have some fun!

# Let's Go!

The climb is hard and your muscles ache. But…just…a little bit farther and you'll coast. One…more…There! You're over the top, and now the green countryside spreads out far below you. You shift your weight forward and relax. Faster and faster you descend, the wind rushing up past your head. The air is cool and it feels great. You sway gently from side to side, balancing, balancing. You round a bend, crouching a bit as you bank your body to make a turn. And then it's over. Far too quickly. You're all the way down.

Wow. It's great being a bird, isn't it?

A bird? Oh. You thought we were talking about riding a bicycle.

### IN CASE YOU'RE WONDERING WHAT A BICYCLE IS…

Webster's Third New International Dictionary defines a bicycle as "a vehicle that has two wheels, one behind the other, a steering handle, and a saddle seat or seats and is usually propelled by the action of the rider's feet upon pedals."

Sorry for the mix-up. Yes, this is a book about bicycles. The mysterious ways they work. Where they came from. And especially how much fun they are.

But first there's something you ought to know—riding your bike is a lot like being a bird, because cycling is very similar to flying. The way you overcome gravity with your muscles, the way you balance, the way you turn, the way you cut through the wind, even the way cycling makes you feel—free as a bird.

People noticed this right from the beginning. A magazine article from 1896 noted that one of the first things people say when they learn to ride a bike is, "It's just like flying!"

3

Or maybe it's like what a five-year-old from California said one hundred years later: "Bikes make me feel like I'm running in the air, like I'm riding a flying chair."

## Sort of a Dream Come True

Ask your friends what they'd do if they had magic powers. At the top of the list? Flying. A teacher once collected a list of her students' wishes:

"I wish I could fly and play with my cousins all day."

"I wish I could fly wherever I wanted to."

"I want to have wings to fly."

"I would make people fly."

"I would love to fly, and I think it would be really cool."

Well, maybe you never thought of it this way, but if you have a bike, you can experience a lot of the fun and freedom of flying, and you never have to leave the ground.

### He Loved Bikes, Yeah, Yeah, Yeah

"As a kid I had a dream—I wanted to own my own bicycle. When I got the bike I must have been the happiest boy in Liverpool, maybe in the world. I lived for that bike. Most kids left their bikes in the backyard at night. Not me. I insisted on taking mine indoors, and the first night I even kept it by my bed."—John Lennon of the Beatles

# It's a Bike! It's a Plane!
## The Bicycle, the Wright Brothers, and the Airplane

*"If you can control a bicycle and prevent it from crashing, you've mastered some of the principles necessary to fly an airplane."*

—Robert Petersen, park ranger and historian, Dayton Aviation Heritage
National Historical Park (site of the Wright brothers' bicycle shop, 1896)

**Y**our bicycle has a very strong connection to the airplane. In fact, it was bike riding, bike parts, and money from selling bikes that helped the Wright brothers of Dayton, Ohio, invent the airplane.

When the Wrights bought their first bicycles in 1892, Orville fell in love with racing, while Wilbur preferred long, slow rides in the country. Both loved mechanical things and found that they were very good at fixing bicycles. Next thing you know, they opened a bicycle repair shop, and later began building and selling their own brands of bicycles—the Wright Van Cleve and the Wright St. Clair.

*Around Dayton, Orville was known as a "scorcher"— a common nickname for early bicycle racers, who got teased for "scorching" the roadways with their speed. Before cars were common, bicycles were the fastest mechanical way for an individual person to get around.*

They made so much money fixing and selling bikes that they were able to move on to other mechanical things—like flying machines.

Because they studied bikes, the Wrights understood how balancing works. And they understood that bicycles, like birds, need to lean when they turn. The Wrights decided that a flying-machine pilot would have to balance and lean a plane—he or she couldn't just sit there and ride. This knowledge of bicycle balancing and leaning had a lot to do with the success of their airplane design.

Owning a shop full of bicycle parts helped, too. In the summers, the shop was described as a "madhouse," with people coming in the front door to buy bikes, and the Wrights in the back room trying to invent an airplane. Imagine the scene at *your* local bike shop—especially if you had never seen an airplane before! *WHAT are those guys doing?*

*Wilbur was in his bike shop idly talking to a customer and wiggling the flat box of a bicycle part when the idea hit him—wiggling a plane's wings might help it balance.*

To test their early ideas about flight, Wilbur and Orville attached wing parts to a bicycle. They'd ride up and down the street in front of their shop as fast as they could to see what wings would do in the wind.

*After they invented the airplane, the Wrights sold their bike business. It eventually became part of the well-known Huffy Bicycle Company.*

The Wrights used bicycle chains and gears to run their planes' propellers, and bicycle frames to support the propellers. They pulled on lines made of bicycle spoke wire to wiggle the wings and make the plane balance and turn. And as it was taking off, the whole plane rode on the hubs of bicycle wheels rolling on a rail. Nick Engler, a builder of flying-machine replicas in Dayton, said there were hundreds of individual bicycle parts on the Wright brothers' planes.

When bicycle sales slowed down every fall, the Wrights took their bicycle/airplane parts to the soft sand dunes of North Carolina to test their ideas. They did this for four years. To get around in the sand, they even invented the world's first beach bike with big balloon tires. Finally, on December 17, 1903, the Wrights' fragile contraption of bicycle parts, wood, cloth, and metal lifted off the ground under its own power. Cycling was no longer "just like" flying—it *was* flying.

*The Wrights built a total of about two hundred bicycles. Only five remain, and they're all in museums, including the Henry Ford Museum and Greenfield Village in Dearborn, Michigan, and the U.S. Air Force Museum in Dayton, Ohio.*

# The Bicycle Balancing Act
## How and Why Your Bike Stays Up

*"Balancing a bicycle is a feedback process, just like balancing a yardstick upright in the palm of the hand."*

—John S. Allen, author, *The Complete Book of Bicycle Commuting*

**D**id a bird teach you to ride your bike? Probably not. But that's just because you didn't ask.

Watch how a bird flies. To take off, go higher, or go faster, the bird flaps its wings. When you want your bike to take off, go up a hill, or go faster, you pedal. Then, after a while, a bird will glide. You and your bike? You coast. Flapping and pedaling, gliding and coasting.

Cool, huh? But that's only the beginning. Watch the bird closely as it's gliding.

### SOUND FAMILIAR?

**W**ords often sound different when you hear them in different languages, but not the word *bicycle*. It comes from the Latin word *bi*, meaning "two," and the Greek word *kyklos*, meaning "wheel," and it's a word you can recognize in many languages.

Albanian: biçikletë

Arabic: bisiklaat

Czech: bicikl

Danish: cykel

Esperanto: bicikleta

French: bicyclette

Italian: bicicletta

Norwegian: sykkel

Portuguese: bicicleta

Romanian: bicícleta

Serbo-Croatian: bicikl

Slovak: bicykel

Spanish: bicicleta

Swahili: baisikeli

Swedish: cykel

Tagalog: bisikleta

Turkish: bisiklet

Every few seconds it'll twitch or wiggle its wings. Know what the bird is doing? Balancing. All during flight, the bird adjusts its wings and shifts its weight to stay on course and upright. This was the action that those bike-riding Wright brothers noted.

It's similar when you ride your bike. You actually stay up and balance by twitching and wiggling your handlebars the whole time you're riding. You tug a quarter of an inch to the right, then to the left, then maybe to the left again, then to the right. You don't even know it, but when your brain senses that the bike is beginning to fall over—even the tiniest little bit—you automatically twitch the handlebars in that direction. The bike's reaction? It leans a little in the opposite direction. You also wiggle your body weight back and forth constantly to help you balance.

## NUMBER OF BICYCLES IN THE WORLD

About one billion—one for every six people. China has the world's biggest population and the most bicycles—about 270 million. The United States is next with about 100 million.

Why don't you realize you're doing this balancing act? Because when you're learning to ride a bike, your body opens new pathways connecting your brain, your inner ears (where your sense of balance begins), and your muscles. Then your brain teaches your body to do this wiggly balancing act automatically. That's why it takes a little time and practice to learn to ride. In a way, your brain begins to treat the bike like part of your body. Once the pathways are open, they don't close. A bird doesn't forget how to fly, and you don't forget how to ride.

### You Turn Like a Bird, Too

Watch a bird as it circles above. Are the bird's wings parallel to the ground or do the wings lean in the direction of the turn? Of course they lean in the direction of the turn. A bird does this naturally. And so does a person riding a bicycle, by shifting his or her weight. In fact, except at the slowest speeds, it's impossible for a bird or a bicycle to make a turn without leaning. Scientists have found that if a bike rider wants to make a right turn, the first thing he or she usually does is twitch the handlebars, amazingly, to the *left*. This forces the bike to begin leaning to the right. Once the bike is leaning to the right, the rider then does what you might expect— steers and leans to the right. (Just switch all these directions around for a left turn.)

## The Myth of the Gyroscope

For a while some scientists thought the main reason that bicycles balance was because of gyroscopic inertia (JI-ro-skopic ih-NER-shuh). That's the force that keeps a toy top or a gyroscope spinning in one place, or a coin rolling along the floor. They thought a bicycle's spinning wheels kept it from falling over. In 1970, British scientist David Jones tried to build an "unrideable bicycle." It had both a regular front wheel and another wheel, slightly smaller, right next to it. The second front wheel spun in the opposite direction to cancel out any gyroscopic forces. Surprise! The bike was quite rideable, and Jones decided that gyroscopic inertia didn't have much to do with a person balancing a bike. Wiggling the wheel is really the key.

### Professor Kickstand's Cycling Advice

**Q.** Dear Professor: I have the world's most uncomfortable bicycle seat. Is there anything I can do to solve the problem?
—Ralph P., Sopchoppy, FL

**A.** Dear Ralph: Absolutely. Ride to a neighborhood creek and collect several dozen small rocks—about an inch across is the right size. Now stuff the back pockets of your pants with the rocks, as many as can fit. Then climb aboard your bike and ride for one hour or ten miles, whichever comes first. Get off the bike, empty your pockets (be sure to put the rocks in a safe place where no one will trip over them), and get back on your bike. Your seat will immediately feel more comfortable. Some riders may need to repeat the procedure for best results.

Old-timers who rode on streets with streetcar tracks knew plenty about the need to wiggle their wheels for balance. If they accidentally dropped a wheel into the track, their wiggle room—and their balance—were gone. *Boom!* Instant dump. And look out! The trolley's coming!

### Think You're Riding in a Straight Line?

Think again. There's an easy way to show the wheel-wiggling that takes place when you're riding your bike. Just ride through a puddle when the rest of the pavement is dry. After you come out of the puddle, go as straight as you can at a slow rate of speed. Then go back and look at your wet tracks on the pavement. You'll see plenty of wet wiggles no matter how straight you thought you were going.

### Hey, What About Unicycles and Riding with No Hands?

Oh, there's still plenty of wiggling and twitching going on. You're just doing it, as they say, by the seat of your pants. . . .

# Did Someone Say Flying?
## The BMX Experience

*"If you're on a bike, you're still a kid. I'm not going to grow up anytime soon."*

—Jason Suchan, a pro BMXer who built $4,000 worth of jumps and ramps in his parents' backyard, quoted in the *Detroit Free Press*

**O**kay. So you don't need to leave the ground to feel like you're flying. But what if you really WANT to? That's why BMX was invented. Back in the 1960s, adults would make dirt piles in empty lots and bounce and fly their motorcycles over the bumps just for fun. They called it "motocross," short for "motorcycle cross-country." When the motorcycles went home, guess who took over? Kids on bikes soon had their very own sport called Bicycle Motocross, or BMX. Trained BMXers ride hard, jump high, crash plenty, and need really strong bikes and special safety equipment to survive the pounding.

Motorcycle companies made some of the first bicycles for BMX, and they looked kind of like motorcycles. The first factory-made bicycle to look like current BMX bikes showed up about 1975.

In 1983, BMX style really took off when the movie *E.T.* showed kids hauling a big-eyed alien around on a bike—and escaping with him by flying into the night sky. Famous movie director Steven Spielberg still uses the "BMX against the moon" as the symbol for his movie company. And then in 1986, the movie *Rad* showed kids all the cool tricks BMX bikers could do.

In 1995 came serious fun. That's when the X Games brought BMX competition to a nationwide audience, and big money prizes to top winners like Dave Mirra.

Today, a kid's first real bike usually has BMX style. That's because BMX bikes use twenty-inch wheels—six or seven inches smaller than a typical adult bike, and perfect for a kid. Most are just used as everyday bikes, and though they're not really great for traveling long distances, they're fine for zipping around the neighborhood. To do a lot of jumping, though, you'll need something more than the typical discount- or toy-store bike with BMX style—real BMX bikes from bike shops have strong frames and wheels that can stand up to all those hard landings.

## Six Ways to BMX

**Just Plain Riding** Ninety-five percent of all kids ride BMX bikes just because they're fun, fast, and built to last. They don't do any extreme tricks. They just ride their bikes for fun and to get places. It's like basketball shoes. Most kids wear them, but hardly any kids play for the NBA.

**Dirt Jumping** This is where BMX started, and it's just what it sounds like—riding and jumping the bike over dirt piles. It's as dirty and dangerous as crashing into the dirt can be.

**Vert** or **Ramp** From a simple piece of wood propped up with rocks, to huge structures made by real carpenters, ramps give BMX bikes a way to take off. And once the bikes are in the air, tricks get more and more complex. The best riders can do flips, spin their bikes around several times, and land with a "so what?" look on their faces. BMX ramps are used by skateboarders and skaters, too.

**Street or Freestyle** This style is pretty much up to the rider—jumping over obstacles, jumping onto benches, sliding down rails. Freestyle bikes often have pegs sticking out from the axles. Riders can stand on the pegs or grab them as they do tricks. Or sometimes they use the pegs to grind—skid along the edge of a wall or along a rail. In competition, this style of riding is sometimes called "Park" because it's performed on a prepared course similar to a skate park.

**Downhill** This style was first introduced as a race at the 2001 X Games. Imagine riding your BMX down a bumpy mountainside and using the bumps as takeoff ramps the whole way. Gravity is so much fun.

**Flatland** Though this type of riding takes place on the ground—no flying off ramps or dirt piles—it's just as wild. Riders climb all over their bikes as they ride, hardly touching the pedals. Sometimes they'll ride only on the back wheel, like a unicycle. Sometimes they'll tip the bike onto the front wheel, stand on the pegs, and bounce on the wheel like a pogo stick. Some of it looks crazy, but all of it looks like fun.

> **BMX Quiz**
>
> *If you hear someone talking about "big air," they*
> 1. *are British and are commenting on someone's "do."*
> 2. *had a jumbo-size bean burrito for lunch.*
> 3. *spanked a bombin' cross-up off a vert launch.*

## Learning to Fly

To begin to understand the trick side of BMX, you need to see it in action. A good place to start is watching videos with titles like *How to Dirt Jump* and *BMX Basics*. These will show and tell you about the safety equipment you need and how to get started. To see BMX live, have your folks take you to a track in your area, where kids compete in both racing and jumping. To find a nearby track, just ask at your local bike shop. You can also contact the national groups that support BMX— National Bicycle League, (800) 886-BMX1, www.nbl.org; or American Bicycle Association, (480) 961-1903, www.ababmx.com. They have lists of all the tracks and also run national competitions.

> **The Other Meaning of the Word**
> *Bicycling: to move a baby's legs up and down to relieve gas pains.*

There are also camps where national champions teach kids how to really catch air. To learn to fly and do flips, you need a safe way to land at first. Camps and some tracks have huge foam pits that BMXers can fall into while they're learning.

BMX as an organized sport is getting bigger and bigger—in some places rivaling kids' baseball and soccer leagues in popularity. Professionals like Dave Mirra make a living out of winning competitions and endorsing products. There is even talk of someday making BMX an Olympic event. Hey, you! Yes, you! Reading this! Want an Olympic gold medal? Start riding!

### And Now a Word from Our Corporate Lawyer

Seriously, guys, BMX riding and performing flying stunts are—by their nature—dangerous activities that can result in serious injury or death. They cannot be made perfectly safe, no matter what. Don't try them without proper training and all the right safety gear.

# On Top of It All
## The Mountain Bike

*"I go mountain biking in the wilderness and come upon this incredible vista. I suddenly realize that the universe is so big and my problems are so minuscule."*

—From a survey about mountain bikes by Pennsylvania State University students

**M**ountain bikes have been around for only about twenty years, but they are now by far the most popular full-sized bike. Of every ten full-sized bikes sold, eight are mountain bikes. Most people never take them into the mountains—they just like how they look: rugged and tough.

Good ones *are* rugged and tough. With their twenty-six-inch wheels, they're like big cousins of BMX bikes, with stronger parts than other types of bikes. And they can go where other bikes can't, like up mountain paths, over logs, through streams. Most have gears that let you choose from at least eighteen different settings. When you're struggling up a steep dirt trail, you can choose a setting that lets you put more power into each pedal push. On level ground, or when riding downhill, you can choose less power but more speed.

Mountain bikes can be heavy, and their fat, knobby tires take extra work to pedal on paved roads. They're not the best bikes for long trips, but their ability to go just about anywhere is a big plus.

Some mountain bikes have springs or other cushion devices to help smooth out the bumps, just like in a car. Sometimes the whole bike frame is part of the system. These shock-absorbing systems can make bikes faster, mostly because going downhill on rough ground is much more comfortable.

In one way, mountain biking has a great safety advantage over regular street biking—it gets you away from car traffic. Just watch out for those logs, stumps, loose gravel, cliffs, and bears. Oh, and a guy riding in a national park once had a wildcat chase him down and leap on his back. Maybe the cat just wanted a ride. . . .

15

### *Really* Mountain Biking

As of August 2000, the highest anyone ever rode a mountain bike is 22,992 feet up on the Mustagh Ata mountain in China. To set the record, Martin Adserballe of Denmark and Siegfried Verheijke and Luc Belet of Belgium carried their bikes most of the way up through the snow and cleared a forty-five-foot riding path in a flat area.

### Check Your Brakes!

Hawaii's Haleakala volcano is 10,000 feet high, and has a crater that's bigger than Manhattan and a mountain bike trail that winds thirty-eight miles down along its side. Believe it or not, it's considered an easy trip—it's only necessary to pedal for about 1,200 feet the whole way down. For the rest of the three-hour trip you're just coasting and braking. And smiling.

### Take the Long Way Home

The world's longest continuous mountain biking route is the Great Divide Mountain Bike Route. Fully mapped in 1998, it winds 2,470 miles through the entire length of the Rocky Mountains, from Canada to Mexico. The record for riding the whole thing is eighteen days. Most people take at least two months.

### Mountain Biking Dot Com

To get all the current information about mountain biking, just go on an Internet search engine and type in the words *mountain bike association* or *mountain biking association*. From the flatlands of Indiana to the peaks of Colorado, there are local mountain bike clubs that tell you just where to ride.

# 5 Road Runners
## The Road Bike

*"It never gets easier, you just go faster."*
—Greg LeMond

These bicycles are fast, lightweight, and they're the best traditional type of bike for long, long rides on paved roads. Often called "racing bikes," their wheels are usually twenty-seven inches across. For about twenty years before mountain bikes came along, the road bike was the most popular full-sized bicycle. They're still the favorite of serious racers and people who take long bicycle tours. Races like the Tour de France are loaded with them.

A road bike almost always has "dropped" handlebars that curl downward. By holding on to these, the rider can push down harder with his or her legs and put more *oomph* into the pedals. These handlebars also keep the rider in a crouched position so there's less wind to cut through (more about that in Chapter 9). Some road bikes also have "aero bars" that stick upward off the handlebars. These let riders change positions and bring their arms closer together for an easier time with the wind.

*A typical road bike has about 1,275 parts.*

**Three reasons to buy a $4,000 road bike**

1. The salesperson says it's twice as fast as a $2,000 road bike.
2. It comes with a free kickstand.
3. They're out of $5,000 road bikes.

Everything about a good road bike is designed to be lightweight. The lightest ones you can buy in a regular bike store weigh only sixteen to twenty pounds (about the weight of two gallons of milk). The very lightest usable road bike as of the year 2000 was eleven pounds.

Lightness helps especially when you're starting out or going up hill. The best, most expensive lightweight bikes are made of aluminum or special metals like titanium or even nonmetals like carbon fiber. The tires are skinny and pumped hard with air to make them roll more easily. The lightweight and skinny tires make road bikes fast and easy to pedal, but they're a bad choice for banging around off-road.

## From Sea to Shining Sea

About ten thousand people a year cross the United States on bicycles, usually road bikes. They almost always go from west to east so they'll get over the Rocky Mountains early and then have the wind at their backs as they ride across the Great Plains. No one is sure who was the youngest cross-country rider, but we do know the first—

> **Got Bucks?**
> The most expensive road bike listed by roadbikereview.com in 2003 was the Ochsner Rhine, priced at $6,599.

Thomas Stevens in 1884. He rode about 3,500 miles from Oakland, California, to Boston, in 103 days, often following railroad tracks. An average cross-country bicycle trip now takes about fifty days.

## Professor Kickstand's Cycling Advice

**Q.** Dear Professor: I like a little music while I ride, but the batteries never last on my little headset radio. Do you have any ideas about providing musical entertainment on a bicycle?

—Barbie T., Skiddy, KS

**A.** Well, Barbie, everyone loves kazoo music, don't they? Now imagine enjoying kazoo music whenever you ride. There's no need to use your hands, you can play any song that pops into your head, it fits in your pocket, and best of all—no batteries! If you want music while you ride, the kazoo is the instrument for you!

# 6 Where the Mountain Meets the Road

## The Hybrid Bike

*"A hybrid is the answer to the question: What would you get if a road bike married a mountain bike and they had kids?"*

—Bob Heath, on www.cyclingsite.com

The word *hybrid* (HIGH-brid) means "a blend of two different things." A hybrid bike blends some of the speed and lightness of a road bike with some of the ruggedness of a mountain bike. It does a lot of things well, and it's great for people who like to ride, but probably aren't going to race, or ride a hundred miles a day, or bump down a dry creek bed in the Rocky Mountains. A hybrid will go places, like bumpy roads or meadows, where you wouldn't want to ride a thin-tired road bike. And it's more comfortable on the road than a knobby-tired mountain bike. Also, the handlebars are higher than those on a road bike, so a hybrid is ridden with the body more upright. It's easier to watch the countryside going by, and very pleasant. If your folks ever say, "Geez, I wish I had a new bike," show them this page. Over the past ten years or so, bicycle brakes and gear shifting have greatly improved, and hybrids take advantage of it all. If your folks get a chance to ride a hybrid, chances are they'll want one. You might even get some new riding buddies.

> *Hybrids usually have handlebars that let you sit upright and wheels that are twenty-seven inches across.*

> ### Extra Iron in the Diet
> *Michel Lotito of France has made news for over forty years by eating crazy things like metal and rubber. It is said that since 1966 he has eaten a total of eighteen shredded bicycles. His appetite for airplanes is not as strong, though. He's eaten only one Cessna.*

## JUST ROLLING ALONG: THE CRUISER BIKE

If you ride a lot where it's flat or almost flat—maybe by the beach or on the plains or in a city—a cruiser will get you where you're going without a lot of fuss. Forget road racing or hill climbing; cruisers are really designed for comfort, with big seats, wide handlebars, and fat tires that serve a lot of purposes. They let you bump over curbs or get through sand, but they're also designed for smooth riding on pavement. There's not a lot to break or get out of adjustment on a cruiser, so they're a favorite of bike rental companies. They just sort of do their job, cruising along happily without a lot of excitement. Okay, we'll say it. They're boring. All right? BORING! And that's why some people insult them. They call them names like clunkers, bombers, trashers, and mashers. So rude! The next time you see a cruiser, be kind. Someday a cruiser may be kind to you. . . .

# How Your Bicycle Got Here
## History on Two Wheels

*"Whoever invented the bicycle deserves the thanks of humanity."*
—Admiral Lord Charles Bereford, British naval hero

**S**o today we have bikes built to fly off ramps and climb mountains and cross continents. We're used to them. But if you stop and think, it's still a crazy idea— humans riding around on two wheels, balancing like birds. Where did this idea come from? Who first thought of it?

### Sketchy Beginnings

Did the people who built the pyramids also build the first bicycles? Maybe. Historians say drawings found in three-thousand-year-old Egyptian tombs show machines that may be bicycles. We do know that the Egyptians used wheels with spokes. Connect two of these together and what do you have? A wild ride down a pyramid, that's what.

And then there's Leonardo da Vinci, one of the world's greatest artists, thinkers, and inventors. He sketched a lot of things in his notebooks, including flying machines and military tanks. In 1490, he sketched something that might have been a bicycle or a tricycle. But some historians think it might just have been a cart to carry a cannon.

Another drawing of a possible da Vinci bicycle even has pedals and a chain. A closer scientific look showed that the two wheels were probably drawn in the 1490s, but that the pedals, chain, and the rest of the bike were drawn much later by a jokester. People still argue that the drawing is real, though. It even inspired a full-sized model that is sometimes seen at da Vinci exhibitions.

And what should we think about the church window in Stoke Poges, England, from 1642? It shows a naked boy blowing a horn and sitting on a wheeled vehicle that's flying on a cloud. An early vision of the bike/flying connection? Probably not. But it sure is fun to think about. What *is* that kid doing?

### Days of the Hobbyhorse

Some historians believe the first bicycle appeared in 1791, while George Washington was president. It was introduced in France by the Comte de Sivrac (kont-duh-see-VROCK) and looked sort of like the contraption in the Stoke Poges window. It had wheels but no pedals and no steering—you just sat on a wooden bar and ran. It was fun, and people called it the *célérifère* (sill-ih-ree-FAIR), which means "swift-moving."

In 1817, a German baron named Karl von Drais wanted to ride a *célérifère* along twisty forest paths, so he invented steering. It was a very big deal. With steering, bikes could now be balanced by the rider and go downhill as fast as a galloping horse. Von Drais named the new bike the *Draisienne* (dray-zee-EN) and became famous showing it all over Europe. In England, the new steerable bike became known as the hobbyhorse, and rich people began buying them for fun.

### Then Came Pedals

By the 1820s, people knew very well how to use cranks and levers to turn wheels. The steamboat had already been invented and all kinds of waterwheels and windmills had been around for centuries. But a hobbyhorse? People were still afraid to take their feet completely off the ground to pedal. So they used their hands! A hobbyhorse built by Lewis Gomphertz in England in 1821 had a lever that you pulled back and forth with your hands while you ran along with your feet on the ground.

It must have looked silly, but it worked—in France they started using this vehicle to deliver the mail. The French called it the *vélocipède* (vih-LO-sih-ped), which means "fast-footed."

The first real foot-pedaled bicycle was invented in 1839 by a Scottish blacksmith named Kirkpatrick Macmillan. His pedals were more like levers, but for the first time, a bicycle moved with the rider's feet completely off the ground. Made with a blacksmith's touch, the Macmillan Velocipede was a sturdy bike that could be ridden long distances. It worked well, but it did not receive much attention outside of Scotland.

*One third of all invention patents applied for in the 1890s involved bicycles in some way. An example was suction cups on pedals to keep the rider's shoes in place.*

In 1861, Pierre Michaux (mee-SHOW), a French carriage maker, had an idea. Put a simple crank on each side of a *vélocipède*'s front wheel—the first real bicycle pedals! If you ever rode a "Big Wheel" toy bike when you were a little kid, you know how these pedals worked. Unlike Macmillan, Michaux gained a lot of attention pedaling along the streets of Paris. It was the simple, easy solution that the world had been waiting for. Everyone wanted to try it, and that's when bicycle manufacturing really began.

Soon thousands of people were pedaling *vélocipèdes* in Europe and America. But remember, roads at this time were for horses and wagons, and *vélocipèdes* had metal strips for tires. Riding was fun, but very bumpy. The *vélocipède* soon earned a new nickname—the "boneshaker."

## About Those Big Wheels

*The materials used in the average car could be used to make one hundred bicycles.*

Because the pedals on a boneshaker connect directly to the front wheel, one turn of the pedals equals one turn of the front wheel. The bigger the wheel, the farther each turn of the pedal takes you. So guess what happened? They started making boneshaker front wheels huge. Soon the front wheels were five feet across. Pedaling just once could take you more than fifteen feet down the road! These weird new bikes were very fast and exciting. Because the back wheel wasn't connected to the pedals, it could be small to save weight. The small wheel/big wheel combination looked funny. It reminded the

British people of a small coin (a penny) and a large coin (a farthing) rolling down the street, and the bikes were nicknamed "penny farthings." First seen in 1869, they became extremely popular when British engineer James Starley began selling the lightweight "Ariel" in 1871.

Penny farthings were dangerous. Hitting a rut or stopping quickly could easily flip the whole bike forward, throwing you over the handlebars, over the five-foot wheel, and onto your head. Talk about flying . . . Ouch! And since your feet could not touch the ground, you could not just sit still on a penny farthing—you had to keep moving. It became a sign of bravery and skill to ride a penny farthing, and the 1870s and 1880s must have been very brave decades. By 1880, penny farthings were found around the world, including about thirty thousand in the United States. At first they were used mainly for sport by wealthy people.

## And Then It Got Safer

Penny farthings were THE bike for about fifteen years, from 1870 until about 1885. But bicycle makers wanted to design a safer, cheaper bike that anybody could ride—not just the daring and wealthy. They realized they didn't need to attach the pedals directly to the front wheel—the pedals could turn the rear wheel through gears and a chain. What's more, by combining large gears and small gears, they could turn the pedals once and make the back wheel turn three or four times. Now it was possible for a bike with small wheels to go twenty-five feet or more with one turn of the pedals—farther than a penny farthing ever could! There was no need to sit on top of a huge wheel anymore. Now the rider could sit and pedal between two wheels of the same size. Stopping quickly was no longer a problem. Climbing aboard was no longer a problem. The thing rode better and faster, too!

*During World War II, only one company in the United States—Columbia—was allowed to make bicycles. America needed the rest of its steel to make war materials.*

The design was patented in 1870, and the first successful chain-driven bicycle was introduced in England in 1885 by John Kemp Starley, whose uncle James had built penny farthings. The new bike was called the Rover Safety Bicycle, and the idea took the world by storm. "Safety" bikes took over as the most popular bicycles, and penny farthings got a new name. They were now called "ordinaries" because they were nothing special anymore.

Safety bikes changed the world. Remember—in 1885 there still weren't any real cars. With a safety bike just about anyone could ride quickly, smoothly, and safely, much farther than ever before, so more people wanted them. When companies make more of something, the price comes down. While a penny farthing might cost over $300, a safety bike was about $85. That was still a lot of money (over $2,000 in today's money), but it was affordable to a greater number of people.

**Sheldon Brown Knows All**

*Want to see wacky bikes, learn how to play bicycle polo, or get helpful hints on helmet decor? Check out Sheldon Brown's Links to Bicyclists, Localities, Organizations, and Services at www.sheldonbrown.com. You can find just about anything and everything about bicycles there. As a kid, Sheldon Brown made money by building and selling bikes from scrap parts. Today he works in a bike shop and updates his amazing Web site, which seems to contain every bicycle link in the world. Cyclists, museums, races, parts, ideas, jokes—it's all there.*

Now people could work, shop, and socialize farther from home. Women in long dresses who couldn't ride a penny farthing had no problem climbing aboard a safety bike. Kids could ride them for fun. The safety bike expanded people's lives, and things would never be the same. Within a few years, over four hundred factories were building bicycles—and that was just in America!

## Making a Good Thing Better

The design of the safety bike was so good that most bicycles still work the same way today. In fact, John Kemp Starley could climb on your bike and pedal away, no problem. He wouldn't find that many changes, either, since some "modern" improvements occurred in his lifetime. The first big improvement came right away—inflatable rubber tires—invented at the same time as the safety bike. Riding on air made the ride much smoother. In 1889, designers figured out how to make a bike "coast" or glide (keep the bike moving forward while the pedals remain still). And they invented the coaster brake, which stops a bike when the rider pushes the pedals backward.

A bicycle craze hit America. By 1889, there were already 200,000 safety bikes on the road. By 1899, there were 1,250,000.

## Beep, Beep!

Soon after 1900, two new vehicles came along to capture the world's attention—the car and the motorcycle. By 1920, riding a bicycle seemed almost old-fashioned, and advertisements spread the idea that if you weren't interested in cars and motorcycles, you weren't cool. It became less common for adults to ride bicycles—bikes became something for kids.

To try to recapture attention, bike makers began producing bicycles that looked more like motorcycles. They piled on heavy fenders and even fake gas tanks! From the 1930s into the 1960s, you could buy bikes with built-in headlights, taillights, and horn buttons. What this stuff really added to bikes was weight. Those big cruisers weighed up to seventy pounds, twice as much as today's average bike. Imagine trying to pedal that up a hill!

At the same time, in Europe, adults still used the bicycle for transportation, mostly because cars and gas were expensive. Europeans kept their bikes lightweight and even came up with ways to switch gears so they could climb hills more easily.

In the 1970s, in America, gasoline started to become expensive, and car-driving adults took new interest in these lightweight bikes that could zip up hills. There was also new interest in health and fitness. Americans started buying so many bikes that for a while in the seventies there was a bike shortage.

Then in the 1980s, the mountain bike took over, with its tough capabilities and looks. Now we're able to ride our bikes just about anywhere. In a way, we've gone back to 1817 and Baron von Drais, who invented bicycle steering so he could ride through the woods.

## WHEN THE WORLD WENT BANANAS

If you were growing up in the sixties or seventies, your bike would probably have had a big banana seat and high butterfly handlebars. Groovy, baby. The style started in California, inspired by the look of custom motorcycles.

Kids at first built their own banana bikes, using seats and handlebars borrowed from the sport of bicycle polo, where adults knocked balls around a field with mallets and needed big seats and big handlebars to fit on their little bikes.

***Even Better Than Flying on Air Force One***

*"Nothing compares with the simple pleasure of a bike ride."*
*—John F. Kennedy, who was president when the first banana bikes were introduced*

The kids found that their new seats and handlebars let them shift their weight back and pull their front wheels into the air very easily. It was called "popping a wheelie." It was new. It was cool. It was California.

Bicycle companies started selling their own banana bikes, and for the next ten or so years, Schwinn Sting-Rays and other high-risers ruled the road. The factories added more and more stuff, like stick shifts and "dragster" tires and tall "sissy" bars on the back. Girls' bikes came with "flower power" decals and wild colors.

The fad faded around 1976 when the U.S. Consumer Product Safety Commission said that banana bikes were more unstable than other types of bikes and were involved in more accidents.

Collectors still love them, and companies sometimes bring back "retro" editions. Today, especially in California, there's a similar style of homemade bike called the "low-rider."

The banana bike may be history, but it was the acrobatic wheelies and fun of the banana bike in the sixties and seventies that led directly to the rise of BMX in the 1980s.

# There's Something in the Air
## Aerodynamics and Your Bike

*"He'd fly through the air with the greatest of ease."*
—George Leybourne, 1868

**S**ome words just sound interesting. *Aerodynamics* (air-oh-die-NAM-mix) is one of them. It comes from the Greek words for "powerful air," and it has to do with the motion of air, or how things move through the air.

Although clean air is invisible, it's actually a soup of tiny particles called "molecules." In order to get through these molecules, you have to push them aside, and that takes energy. The larger and flatter the front of an object, the more energy it takes to get through the molecules.

> **Do Not Disturb**
> Good aerodynamics have been described as opening a clean hole through the air, moving through the hole, and letting the hole close again with the least disturbance.

The faster the object tries to move, the more air it has to push. You can feel something similar in water— pull your hand through water slowly and you don't feel much resistance, but pull your hand fast and . . . whew! The water feels heavy. The weight you feel when you're pushing aside air molecules is called air resistance.

Believe it or not, to go one mile on a bicycle, you need to push aside three thousand pounds of air. Anytime you try to do this quickly, it becomes a chore. On a bike, the hard work starts at about ten miles per hour. At twenty miles per hour, you're pushing aside three thousand pounds of air every three minutes! If you're not trained for racing, just moving all this air is 90 percent of your work.

One problem with air resistance is that it increases greatly as you go faster. Just speeding up from twenty miles per hour to twenty-six—the speed of a typical road race—requires double your energy thanks to the increased air resistance.

Now, what's the largest, flattest thing on a bicycle? You! Your body gives a bike all its power, but also gives it most of its air resistance.

That's why bicycle racers go into a "tuck" and crouch down low on their handlebars. To get through the air, they're trying to make themselves as small as possible. But crouching down and bringing their shoulders together creates a problem. It gives the lungs less room to expand with oxygen. And riding a bike is one of the times (huff) you need (puff) a lot of oxygen!

## TESTING YOUR SLICKNESS

**W**ant to find out how much difference your riding position makes? You'll need a bike, a day with no wind, a stopwatch, some chalk, a pencil, a notepad, and—most important—a long, steep, straight hill on a paved road with no traffic. Use the chalk to mark off a starting line and a finish line, at least three hundred feet apart—the farther apart the better. Make sure you'll be able to coast quickly from start to finish without any pedaling or shoving off at all. You need to be able to just pick up your feet and coast. Use the stopwatch to time yourself as you coast, trying a different riding position each time—fully upright, crouched down, shoulders out, shoulders in. Make sure the only thing that changes on each trip down the hill is your riding position, and write down your riding position and time for each trip because it's easy to get mixed up. Try everything, but be sure you can always see where you're going and can work your brakes. At the end you'll know your slickest aerodynamic position and have the beginnings of a pretty slick science-fair project, too!

**99 Percent
of Cyclists Have It. . . .**

*Back in the 1880s, doctors came up with a name for heavy breathing while
bicycling. Now take a deep breath. It's called "velocipedraniavaporina"
(veh-LOSS-ih-peh-dran-ee-ah-vay-por-REEN-ah).*

That's an important part of bicycle race training—finding the best position for a tuck. You want the least air resistance possible, but you still want to be able to breathe freely.

Another aerodynamic trick of racing is called "drafting." The first rider through still air needs to do the most work. Once the air is disturbed, a bike that's following will have an easier time. In races, you'll often see one rider closely following another. The one behind is actually saving energy this way. In team racing, riders will take turns being first during most of the race. At the end, the strongest ones will break away just in time to cross the finish line first.

Birds draft, too. Geese flying in a V-shape are really drafting. They take turns being first while the rest are saving energy.

**He Wheelie Did It!**

*In 1999, Kurt Osburn of California became the first person to ride a bicycle on its back wheel only from coast to coast. For two and a half months he'd wake up in his mobile home, get on his bike, pop a wheelie, and ride front-wheel-up for fifty or so miles. His friends followed along in the mobile home for 2,839.6 miles.*

# Is a "Bent" Bike in Your Future?
## The Recumbents Are coming. Fast.

"The bicycle is a curious vehicle. Its passenger is its engine."

—John Howard, who once rode his bike 152 miles per hour behind a
windscreen on the Bonneville Salt Flats

**Y**our parents may have ridden banana bikes—but will your own kids ride "bent" bikes? "Bent" comes from the last four letters of the word *recumbent* (ree-KUM-bent), from the Latin word for "lie down."

On a recumbent bike, the rider doesn't sit astride a saddle. Instead, he or she leans back in a seat that looks kind of like a lawn chair. Legs are stretched out forward to the pedals. It looks relaxing to ride, and it is. But that doesn't mean it's slow.

In fact, recumbent bikes are *very* fast. Every human-powered land-speed record is held by recumbents. The fastest sprint speed goes up every year, and now it's over eighty miles per hour. In contrast, the sprint record for a bicycle with a more traditional sitting position is just over fifty-one miles per hour.

One reason bents are so fast is aerodynamics. Because the rider sits with legs up, the shape pushing through the air is smaller than it is on a regular bicycle. Plus, on a bent, it's easy to enclose the mechanical parts and the rider with smooth coverings called "fairings." This makes the bike slice through the air like a knife.

Another reason they're fast is leg power. Because the rider leans against a backrest, he or she can force extra power into the pedals. In a test, a ninety-pound boy sat on a regular bike. In a riding position, with his hands on the handlebars, he was able to apply seventy pounds of weight to the pedals. With a firm backrest and his legs stretched out in a recumbent position, he was able to apply almost 150 pounds!

Lung power helps, too. On a bent, the shoulders are back and the lungs are free to expand fully.

Recumbents aren't new. In 1839, the Macmillan Velocipede had a feet-up pedaling position. Other bents came and went for almost a hundred years. Then, in 1934, the International Cycling Union worried that recumbents' speed and aerodynamics were unfair to regular bicycle racers. It banned recumbents and bikes with fairings from official races, and the feet-up idea cooled down.

But now the idea is back. In fact, a whole new group has formed to test and race all kinds of unusual bikes—the International Human Powered Vehicle Association (IHPVA). Interest in fast, comfortable bikes is growing.

Though bents are more expensive then regular bikes, prices are likely to come down as more manufacturers compete to get your business. Chances are you'll ride through the air with your feet up someday.

## Hills? No Hassle

Early bents were heavy and had a reputation for slow hill climbing. New lightweight models have just about solved that problem. Also, recumbents use muscles

differently. Even a champion biker at first may think *This thing is hard to pedal*. It's just that the muscles need some time to adapt. Going down a hill on a bent, even a first-timer will blow by just about any other bike on the road.

## A Little Suction Can Be a Good Thing

Recumbents may have great aerodynamics, but what if you completely eliminate the wind as a factor? You get the fastest bike in the world, that's what. In 1995, Fred Rompelberg rode 166.94 miles per hour on the Bonneville Salt Flats in Utah. He rode behind a racing car with a big windscreen that completely protected him from the wind, so there was no need for a recumbent or a fairing. In fact, blocking the wind created a suction effect that helped pull Fred to his world record. Because bicycle records like this rely on the use of cars, they're not counted as "human-powered" records.

# Getting Squished Can Really Ruin Your Day

## Staying Safe on Your Bike

> "The helmet had several rocks embedded in it that would have otherwise been lodged in my skull!"
>
> —John Mechlin, Ohio bike rider after a major crash

**H**ospitals are not fun. Strangers poking at you. Weird food. Getting up in the middle of the night to take medicine. Going to the bathroom in little plastic containers. And worst of all—hospital gowns that don't close all the way. Do you really want to go through all this just because you rode your bike like a dweeb?

### You Need Your Noggin

The first thing you have to remember is your helmet. The reason is simple. Scientists studied exactly how people get killed and hurt badly on bicycles. About 75 percent of the time it's from a bang on the head. See, your brain controls everything else in your body. Break an arm or a leg, and it's likely you'll still breathe and your heart will still beat. But a brain injury can stop or change everything. In fact, cyclists admitted to hospitals with head injuries are twenty times more likely to die than those admitted without head injuries. Remember this: Helmets can eliminate at least 70 percent of the head injuries suffered in bike crashes. That's why more and more states and towns are requiring that you wear one when you ride.

### Don't Be Driveway Debris

The most dangerous spot for you and your bike is right in front of your house. This is where the average kid enters a roadway most often—sometimes dozens of times a day. When nothing happens the first three hundred times, it's easy to get lazy. It's easy to forget to stop and look for cars, and just zip right out. Then one unlucky day, BAM! You say hello to a truck bumper. This is called the "ride-out accident," and it's one of the most common and dangerous accidents for kids under

## AND NOW A MESSAGE FROM PEDAL PETE, THE SAFETY BUFFALO

Howdy, kids! It's me, Pedal Pete, the Safety Buffalo, here to tell you everything I know about bicycle safety. It's easy. First, put on your helmet, climb aboard your bike, grasp the handlebars firmly, place your feet on the ground, and don't go anywhere. When you get bored, just go into the house, get yourself a snack, and watch TV. Now that's safe biking. This was a message from Pedal Pete, the Safety Buffalo.

thirteen. Don't ever get so lazy and sloppy and comfortable on your bike that you enter any roadway without at least slowing down and looking both ways.

### Did You Know You're Invisible?

Before you go riding in traffic, spend some time watching how your folks drive. They poke at the radio, look at road signs, yell at other drivers, turn around to see what you're doing, talk on a cell phone. No, they're not looking out for bicycles. On roads with four-thousand-pound cars, sixty-five-thousand-pound trucks, and a million distractions, you and your bike are just about invisible. If you ride on the road, ride like your life depends on it. Because it does.

- Riding toward the flow of traffic is one of the most dangerous things you can do. Drivers don't expect you there, and they are likely to turn right into your path. Plus, if your bike is going ten miles per hour and a car is coming toward you at forty miles per hour, your "crash" speed would be equal to fifty miles per hour. *Ouch!* Wrong-way bike riding is the reason for one of every three car/bike crashes.

- Riding the same way as traffic may seem dangerous, because your back is to the cars. It's been proven to be almost FOUR TIMES SAFER than riding against traffic. You should still consider yourself invisible to busy drivers, but if you stay to the right, don't sway back and forth, and leave plenty of room for cars to pass you, you'll probably be okay.

- An especially nasty surprise is called the "car-door crash." It happens when someone in a parked car suddenly opens a car door right in your path. (You're invisible, remember?) It can be like riding into a knife blade. When you're riding past parked cars, look for people's heads inside. It's a clue that a door may open at any moment.

## Professor Kickstand's Cycling Advice

**Q.** Dear Professor: My brother, sister, and I are very clumsy bike riders. We crash and fly off our bikes headfirst at least once a week, and I mean all three of us. That means our family goes through about three bicycle helmets a week. It seems like such a waste to just throw them all away, but our garage is getting full. What should we do?

—Chuck Z., Pahrump, NV

**A.** Dear Chuck: That's easy! Adults love to wear old bicycle helmets as kneepads when they're gardening. Just ask them! Not only that, but old helmets make excellent hanging planters. Just fill the helmet with dirt, throw in a few seeds, and hang the planter by the chin straps on your front porch. The neighbors will think you're so clever. Lastly, there's turtle charity. Turtles who have lost their shells are always on the lookout for old bike helmets to wear on their backs, especially wildly colored ones. Just leave your old helmets on your lawn. Sooner or later a turtle will take them.

## Lighten Up, Will Ya?

Riding in the dark, or when it's almost dark, increases your chances of getting hurt, not just by cars, but by things you might hit. As a rule, don't ride in the dark or at dusk. Today's bikes come with good reflectors on the front, back, wheels, and pedals, but these can only help so much. Putting a bright white light on the front and a blinking red one on the back may help a bit, but it's still not enough. If you ever lose track of time and find the sun going down fast, do whatever you can to be seen as you get yourself home. A little trick is to switch your clothes around and wear your lightest-colored clothes on the outside. Hey, stretching a white T-shirt *over* a dark jacket may look weird, but it's dark out anyway, so who cares?

## About Those Pesky Stop Signs and Traffic Lights

For some reason, many kids on bikes don't think they have to stop at stop signs, obey traffic lights, and follow other traffic rules. News flash: You do. Bikers that don't follow traffic rules make crazy drivers even crazier—and more dangerous. A bike on a road is considered a vehicle, and you have to learn and follow vehicle rules. (And you thought you could wait a few more years for your driver's test. . . .) Every intersection is different, so it's impossible to provide a set of rules here that covers everything. That's why you should never ride the roads without first having a bike-riding adult go with you to help you learn how to make traffic decisions and gain other cycling experience. There is one rule that always applies, though: If you find yourself confused or scared about a traffic situation and you're able to get off your bike safely, an answer might be to walk your bike. A person walking a bike is no longer considered a vehicle. He or she is a pedestrian. Cars are supposed to let pedestrians go first. (But now you need to be careful as a PEDESTRIAN!)

## Before You Go, Stop

Some people just don't know when to stop. Or how to stop. Today's bikes have all kinds of brakes, and you need to get a feel for how a bike stops before you go flying down the road. The biggest difference is between a "coaster," or foot, brake and hand brakes. No doubt every rider who has switched between the two types has felt that weird "oops" feeling when he or she tries to hit the brakes and there's nothing there. There are also big differences between types of hand brakes—some grab instantly, some take longer. Some need equal pressure on both hand brakes, some are better when you squeeze harder on one than the other. The feel of braking can change over time even on the same bike. That's why it's always important before you ride any bike to practice hitting the brakes a few times before you take off. If you hear weird sounds or feel unsafe, be sure to have the brakes checked by a bike shop or an adult.

## Woof!

Dogs like bikes, too. They like to chase them. And that can get nasty if they decide to bite. If a mean dog is chasing you from behind, sometimes you can outrun it, but dogs often lunge at you from the side or from the front. If a dog is going for your leg and you feel you can't outrun it, sometimes yelling can scare it. Some riders say a squirt from a water bottle can surprise and stop an attacking dog. And then there's your bike itself. It can make a pretty good shield. Stop the bike, get off on the opposite side from the dog and hold the bike between you and all the barking and growling. Sometimes you can slowly walk away like this and the dog will lose interest. Other times you may have to do some fancy footwork to keep the dog from coming around or jumping over the bike. Use your bike like a circus lion tamer uses a chair. If you are bitten, go to a doctor or hospital immediately. Make sure your parents know and be ready to tell the police what the dog looks like and where it happened.

## The Gory Details: Some Not-So-Trivial Bike Safety Trivia

- In 1997 in the United States, 225 kids under fourteen were killed in bike accidents. Cars were involved in more than two hundred of these accidents—almost 90 percent.

- Boys are seven times more likely to be killed in bike accidents than girls.

- The most common ages to be killed on a bike are fourteen and fifteen.

- Eighty percent of fatal bike accidents involving kids under age fourteen are caused by the rider's behavior—riding into a street without stopping, turning left or swerving into traffic that's coming from behind, running a stop sign, riding against the flow of traffic, etc.

- Most bicycle-related trips to the emergency room are caused by simple falls (50 percent), followed by hitting an object (29 percent), followed by colliding with a vehicle (15 percent).

- Bicycle-related injuries that most often lead to emergency-room visits include arms/hands (60 percent), legs/feet (47 percent), face (35 percent), head (22 percent), brain injury (7.8 percent), and neck (2.7 percent). The numbers add up to more than 100 percent because visits often involve more than one type of injury.

## Bust Your Helmet, Not Your Head

Just so you know: Wearing a bike helmet is not like wearing a football helmet or a pot on your head. Most of today's bike helmets are good for only one accident—the Styrofoam inside the helmet is designed to crush when the helmet hits something. This crushing action soaks up the energy of the crash before it damages your skull. If you wipe out and bang your head, it's time to buy a new helmet.

# Take a Ride. You'll Feel Better.
## What Riding Does for Your Body and Brain

> "When the spirits are low, when the day appears dark, when work becomes monotonous, when hope hardly seems worth having, just mount a bicycle and go out for a spin down the road, without thought on anything but the ride you are taking."
>
> —Sir Arthur Conan Doyle, author of the Sherlock Holmes stories

Crashes. Scrapes. Bumps. Sometimes it may seem like you'd be healthier NOT riding a bike.

Nope. In fact, riding a bicycle is one of the most healthful things you can do. (As long as you read Chapter 11 first.)

The average elementary-school kid bikes about five hundred miles a year. During every one of these miles, you're building muscles in your legs, arms, wrists, fingers, chest, back—just about everywhere. You're especially building the largest, most powerful muscles in your body—the hamstrings and quadriceps (KWAH-drih-seps) in your thighs, and your calf muscles.

After a hard day of riding, you may feel sore—that's just the muscles repairing, rebuilding, and making themselves stronger.

Probably the most important muscles you exercise on a bike are your heart and lungs. Your heart becomes better at pumping blood, and your lungs become better at using oxygen. The steady rhythm of your legs as you pedal actually helps your heart pump blood.

More blood to your brain means more nutrients to your brain. This can help you think and remember things more clearly. Exercise like bike riding also causes your brain to release proteins called endorphins (en-DOR-fins) into your blood. Endorphins are natural painkillers that travel through your body and help to quiet down excited nerve cells. Worried or angry about something? Bike riding can help you feel better.

## Stretching: The Truth

When you ride your bike, you exercise muscles, but leg muscles can stiffen up. In long races like the Tour de France, muscles can tighten so much that riders have to lower their seats a little bit every day to stay in the right riding position. Now don't go getting out your wrenches. For everyday riding, you can loosen up your important leg muscles before and after a ride—or anytime—by doing these three types of stretches:

- **Moo. Calf Stretch**

  Relax. It has nothing to do with a baby cow. The muscle on the back of your leg, opposite your shin, is called a calf. Stand about two feet from a wall, facing it. Lean forward until both palms are against the wall. Now take a step forward with one leg. The other leg should be stretched out behind you so you feel a gentle tightness, but not pain. Hold this poisition for thirty seconds. Then repeat the whole thing with the other leg.

- **Oink. Hamstring Stretch**

  No, it's not a new pig dance. Hamstrings are long, strong muscles in the back of your thighs, and they easily tighten up. Stand with both feet together, then cross one foot over the other. Then bend forward from your hips, dangling your arms as low as they'll comfortably go. Hold the position for thirty seconds and then repeat with the other leg.

- **Seen a Dinosaur Lately? Quadriceps Stretch**
  Quadriceps are not related to triceratops. Quadriceps are long muscles on the front of your thighs. Stand on one leg, pick your other leg up behind you, and grab your ankle. Pull the ankle gently upward—straight behind you, not off to the side. Hold the position for thirty seconds and repeat with the other leg.

## Take Your Time

Muscles need about thirty seconds to fully release during a stretch. Don't try to stretch too quickly. And don't bounce or try to force muscles to stretch. Just give each muscle a nice, long, smoooooooth stretch. You'll be amazed how good it feels when you're done. Stretching makes your muscles ready for the pushing, bouncing, and bumping they'll feel on a bike ride. You can ride longer with less soreness. Doing the same stretches just after a bike ride can also help keep your muscles from stiffening up and making you sore.

---

*An Important Cycle-Logical Test*

*Please check the box that best describes your feelings about bicycles.*

*Fax your answers to headquarters immediately, if not sooner.*

❑ *Cyclomania: to be obsessed with bicycles*

❑ *Cyclophilia: to be in love with bicycles*

❑ *Cyclophobia: to be afraid of bicycles*

❑ *Cyclostupidity: to be stupid about bicycles*

# Show Your Bike You Care
## Easy Bike Maintenance

> "Before John learned how to be a bicycle mechanic, he trained to be
> a fully licensed airplane mechanic. He can also fix your airplane."
>
> —Pedal Pushers Bike Rental & Repair, Harrison, Idaho

**I**f you had a horse, you'd feed it and brush it and shine its horseshoes with shoe polish every day, right? Right. Sure you would. Well, your bike needs care, too.

Some kids like to tinker with wrenches and screwdrivers and oilcans. There is lots to know about keeping a bike's brakes and gears running right, and every bike is different. Before you go putting oil on a brakepad, losing your brakes and crashing through a fence, please talk to a bike-smart adult about tinkering with your bike.

Whether or not you like to tinker, there are two major things every kid needs to know about bicycle maintenance—keeping the right amount of air in the tires and keeping the seat at the right height.

## The Importance of Air

Let's talk about those rubber doughnuts we roll around on—tires. Isn't it weird that tires are full of air? A Scottish veterinarian named John Dunlop thought of it in 1885, and no one's had a better idea yet. The air keeps the rider separated from every little bump in the road. And it does this while adding hardly any weight to the bike—because it's as light as, well, air.

But imagine what tires go through. Bouncing along and bumping curbs, skidding and grinding against gravel. And on a sunny day, that pavement is HOT! Is it any wonder that air sometimes escapes? It's your job to make sure you're riding on the right amount of air.

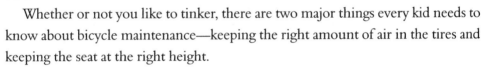
*A bicycle pump is something you'll need to use at least a few times every year. A cheap discount-store pump will last only about a year—get the best one you can afford.*

Too much air can hurt your braking and cornering power—the tires skid too easily if they're too hard.

Not enough air can make the bike difficult to pedal and waste your energy. The right amount of air for each tire is printed on the side of the tire. It says INFLATE TO, and then there's a number. To check your air, you'll need a tire pressure gauge (rhymes with cage), available at any bike shop. Ask an adult to show you how to use the gauge. A bike-shop worker is a good choice.

> *Avoid using gas-station air pumps to fill your tires. In a few seconds they can blow a bicycle tire to smithereens.*

It's also important to have a hand pump. An adult should be able to show you how to use this, too. If you need air, you can pump some in through the valve stem—that black thing sticking up between your spokes. Uncap the valve stem and then pump and check the pressure until you reach the number that's printed on the tire. Too much air? Just touch that little metal thing in the middle of the open valve. Air will come hissing out. Always remember to put the valve cap back when you're done.

## Professor Kickstand's Cycling Advice

**Q.** Dear Professor: Why do my tires lose air if I don't ride my bike for a month or so? —Becky H., Mehoopany, PA

**A.** Dear Becky: It's often a squirrel problem. After a rain, squirrels like to blow-dry themselves with air from bicycle tires. They sneak into the garage, unscrew the valve cap with their teeth, get a little "ffffffft," screw the cap back on, and run away. After a month of this, you've got a flat. To solve the problem, park your bike with the valve stems at the top. Most squirrels won't be able to reach them.

### The Seat of Power

A simple thing you can do to increase your bike's power is to make sure your seat is at the right height. This lets your muscles use their full strength to crank the pedals. You can go farther and faster on the same energy.

To racers, seat height is a science. They experiment on machines that compute how much power they generate, and find exactly the right seat height. As little as one millimeter up or down can make a big difference.

Finding *your* right seat height is even more interesting. Because you're a kid, you're always growing. The right height when school gets out will *not* be the right height at Halloween. You'll need your seat adjusted at least twice a year, so you better learn how to do it. A lot of bikes these days have quick-release clamps that make it easy, but on many bikes you still need a wrench.

What's the right seat height? It's probably a little higher than you think. To find it, push one pedal all the way down. Now put your heel on the pedal and straighten your leg. To keep the bike upright, you'll have to stand on the toes of your other foot or hold on to a wall with your hand. Get off the bike. Adjust the seat up or down until you can sit comfortably with your leg straight and your heel on the pedal when it's all the way down. Do this for both sides. You'll probably have to get on and off the bike a few times to get it right.

Don't think all this heel stuff means you pedal with your heels, or even the middle part of your foot, the arch. Though you measure to your heels, you actually should pedal using the widest part of your foot (the "ball" of your foot). With your foot in this position, your leg will be just slightly bent when the pedal is all the way down. This position lets you get the most power out of your muscles.

The seat may seem too high at first—many kids, especially young ones, prefer to sit with both feet flatly on the ground. You may find you'd rather have your seat somewhere in the middle. However you adjust your seat, give it a chance. It usually takes a few hours of riding for any new position to feel comfortable.

# What's the Difference Between a Bike and an Elephant?

## Carrying Stuff on a Bicycle

> "Bicycles wouldn't be any good as fire engines. Firefighters need lots of special equipment like hoses, ladders, and oxygen tanks when they're fighting fires. How would you carry all of that on a bicycle?"
>
> —From "What If Everybody Rode a Bicycle?," on www.gridclub.com

The answer to the question above is easy. A bicycle doesn't have a trunk! (A bicycle doesn't have huge ears or tusks, either, but that's not the point.) What we're talking about here is carrying stuff on bikes—even though it doesn't have a trunk.

Wouldn't it be great to be able to take your basketball to the park without it falling off and bouncing down the street? Or how about taking a big towel to the pool without getting it tangled in the spokes? Imagine taking every one of your Beanie Babies or video games to your friend's house, and not dropping even one of them in a puddle. It can be done!

### Put It All Behind You

The first step is putting a rear carrier on your bike. These range in price from about $12 to $50, but if you shop around, you can get a decent one for about $20. By itself, a rear carrier doesn't hold much, but it's just the starting point for a whole world of carrying convenience. You'll need some adult help to install the carrier, or any bike shop can do it for you.

Now you need some bungee (BUN-jee) cords to attach things to the carrier. You've probably heard of bungee jumping, right? Well, these are the same basic bungees, but the ones you'll need are only about fourteen inches long and stretch to about twenty inches. They have hooks on both ends. You can get them in any hardware store for a buck or two. Get at least two of them. Note: You need to be careful when stretching bungees because if they slip, the hooks can snap back and hurt you. Always make sure to keep a bungee away from your face while you're stretching it.

The cool thing about bungees is that once you hook them in place, they stretch and let things move a little, but they don't let go. You now have a way to carry small things like doll cases and CD cases. And long things like hockey sticks and baseball bats can easily be carried lengthwise.

## A Crate Is Great

But what about big, bulky, or floppy stuff like skates or towels or basketballs? The answer is a lightweight plastic crate, sometimes called a milk crate or a file crate. You can get these in discount department stores or office supply stores. Just bungee the crate on the carrier and you're ready to go.

*In China, they have shortages of plastic crates, because everybody uses them on their bicycles.*

Another good thing about having a rear carrier on your bike is that it can also hold real saddlebags—these are often used by long-distance bike travelers. Saddlebags put the weight low on the bike, which helps keep it steady.

You can also carry stuff on bikes in a backpack or a messenger bag (an over-the-shoulder bag that bicycle messengers use in cities to carry packages around). But these are really good only for short trips. A backpack should have an extra strap that ties around your waist to keep it steady on your back. Bags sliding around on your back can easily throw you off balance.

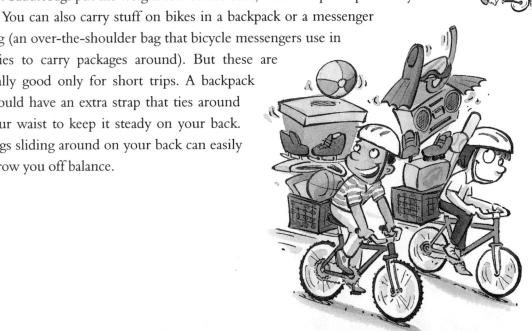

Gadgets and Gizmos
## Cool Accessories/Dumb Accessories

Knock, knock.
Who's there?
Isabelle.
Isabelle who?
Is a bell necessary on a bicycle?

There are lots of things that are not really necessary on a bicycle but still lots of fun to put on.

So what about bells and horns? Well, they've long been sold for safety, but the truth is, if you need to warn somebody that you're coming, your voice does a better job than any little noisemaker. Just yell! But bells and horns can be fun just for their goofiness.

### Other Noisemakers

Speaking of noisemakers, it's always fun to make your bike sound like a motorcycle. Unless you're trying to sneak up on somebody, that is. Years ago, when baseball cards were just throwaway items and people hung wet laundry on clotheslines, kids would clip a baseball card near their wheel with a clothespin. The card would flap against the moving spokes and make a cool *brappa, brappa, brappa, brappa* sound.

*Actual line from the 1980 movie Airplane!: "All right, Striker. You listen and listen close. Flying a plane is no different from riding a bicycle. It's just a lot harder to put baseball cards in the spokes."*

The setup never lasted more than a few minutes, but for a while it sounded like you were riding a motorcycle.

These days every baseball card is treated like a treasure and clothespins are hard to find, but there's an even better way to make a spoke-whacking motorcycle noisemaker. Just get an empty paper-towel roll and flatten it down on one end. This is the end that will flap on the spokes. If you can't find any clothespins around the house, you can still buy them at supermarkets (some people use them to keep potato-chip bags closed) or use some tape. Clip or tape the roll to your front-wheel fork with one end of the roll in contact with the spokes. These rolls make a deeper sound than baseball cards ever did, probably because the round part of the roll acts like an exhaust pipe.

If you want the ultimate Harley-Davidson sound, you have to use balloons. Partially inflate and tie off one or two long, narrow balloons. Tape or clip them to your front-wheel fork and have them loosely touch the spokes. You'll get a rich, satisfying *blawda, blawda, blawda, blawda* sound. For a few minutes, at least, until the balloons explode. Experiment with different inflations and positions for the best sound and longest balloon life.

## Water Bottles

Many bikes these days have a place where you can attach a water-bottle holder.

> **Water Bottles Grossing You Out?**
>
> Rinse the inside of your bottles with minty mouthwash— it kills germs (millions of them! on contact!) and gets rid of the yucky plastic taste, too.

Do it. It's more important than you think. You lose a lot of water through sweat while you're riding a bicycle, but you often don't realize it because the wind dries it up immediately. By the time you feel thirsty, it may be too late to catch up quickly by drinking. Lack of water can lead to weakness, dizziness, and headaches. And that can get in the way of your fun. The trick is to drink *before* you get thirsty.

## Lights

Lights? You really shouldn't be riding at night, period. You really can't trust bicycle lights to help you see or be seen. Also, bouncing around on your bike all the time just about guarantees the light won't work when you want it to. Electrical stuff and bicycles just don't seem to mix. If you really want lights on your bike, get the kind that comes off and can also be used as a regular flashlight. This way you may remember to keep it working and the batteries fresh.

## Flowers and Flags

Flowers and flags are great things to put on your bike, especially for parades, but also for goofing around.

Flowers work well in a plastic vase that you can tape or bungee to the handlebars. Make sure the vase is plastic! No glass, crystal, or china, please!

Want to put flags on your bike? Tape or bungee any flag sticks on the *back* of your bike. Attaching sticks to the handlebars is never a good idea. Hit a pothole and you could have a stick up your nose or in your eye.

Another cool thing to do is wrap your bike in ribbons to mark holidays and events. Use tape to keep the ribbon on. For Halloween, use orange and black. Use your school colors for the first or last day of school. Patriotic holidays? Red, white, and blue. Unless you live in England or France. Then you should use white, blue, and red.

## A Lock. Definitely.

According to *Bicycling* magazine, more than 430,000 bicycles are reported stolen every year in the United States—that's one every 1.2 minutes! About 75 percent of these bikes were left unlocked. So what's the solution 75 percent of the time? Get a lock. You probably don't want to be worrying about a key, though. Get a strong combination lock and either a hardened steel chain or cable. Sometimes you need a U-lock like they use in cities. Local bike shops can make lock recommendations for your bike, depending on how common theft is in your area. Or just check out a bike rack in your neighborhood to see what others are using.

Another accessory you need is a small weatherproof sticker with your name and phone number on it in permanent ink. Put the sticker under your seat

> *Number-one sign that you have a crummy bike: Someone steals your lock but leaves your bike behind.*

## BUT MA, I'LL BE QUIET. HONEST.

Imagine asking your folks to spend money on a toy that just makes noise. That's what the V-RROOM! motor did, back in the sixties. It was a battery-operated fake motorcycle engine that clamped between the pedals of any bicycle and made a loud roaring noise when you turned it on with a plastic key. V-RROOM!

or under your handlebars—somewhere out of sight. If your stolen bike is found, you'll need something to prove that it's yours.

If the underside of your seat is plastic, you should also carve your name into the plastic. The tip of a small ballpoint pen is very hard and works well to engrave plastic. (Works great on aluminum and many other metals, too!)

Then there's the serial number. Somewhere on your bike's frame is a number stamped into the metal. This is called the serial number, and every bike has a different one. Writing this number down and keeping it in a safe place can prevent problems when some creep steals your bike and insists that it's his or hers. "What's the serial number?" is often the first thing the police ask.

# 16 YEE-HAH! It's a Bike Rodeo!
## A Wheel Fun Event

> "Leave your Appaloosa in the stable; all you're gonna need for this
> kind of bronco bustin' is a standard-issue kid's bike."
>
> —Disney's FamilyFun.go.com

**H**ere's a great way to have some rodeo fun without annoying bulls or other large animals. Sometimes kids start these bicycle get-togethers in their neighborhoods, and they grow into events for the whole town. They make great Memorial Day, Independence Day, or Labor Day traditions.

You can do a small version on your own. Just use someone's driveway or an unused basketball court. For a larger version, you might need a school yard or a roped-off parking lot—and adults to help you. Often a large rodeo starts off with a bicycle safety inspection to check brakes, tire conditions, reflectors, nuts and bolts, helmets, etc. Police and recreation departments as well as local insurance companies are always interested in safety, and they often have official bike rodeo guidelines. Adult cycling clubs and groups like the Rotary Club and Jaycees are often glad to help, too. A phone call or two is probably all it will take.

In most rodeo events, you're racing against the clock, so the timekeeper will need a watch that counts seconds. But to really avoid arguments, you'll need a stopwatch. Plastic digital stopwatches are available in sporting-goods departments for a few bucks. Some cool bike rodeo events you can do on your own include:

### The Two-Wheel Twist

The idea is to get through a twisting, zigzag course in the fastest time. You can mark the course with chalk, or put down markers like old plastic milk jugs weighed down with water. Anyone that touches a chalk line or marker is out. The course layout is up to you, but it's good to experiment. You want it to be challenging, but not so challenging that nobody can do it.

## The Straightaway

This event will surprise anyone who hasn't read Chapter 2 and doesn't realize that balancing a bike relies on wiggling the front wheel. Draw two parallel chalk lines about twenty feet long and six inches apart. This is easiest if two kids

stretch a string along the pavement in a straight line while a third kid follows along the string with the chalk. Each rider places his front wheel between the lines at the starting point, and tries to get to the end of the course without touching the lines. It's far harder than it looks. If it's too hard, or if younger kids are racing, you might want to make the lines twelve inches apart.

## The Snail

Get out the camera; you're going to see some fancy balancing! Make a course about three feet wide and ten to twenty feet long. The idea is to travel the length of the course in the *longest* period of time. The only rules are no backtracking and no feet (or other supports) on the ground. Riders can come to a complete stop if they like, start up again, and zigzag as much as they like. Expect to see legs flying and handlebars twitching in all directions as riders try to balance. Without fast-forward motion, all the twitching and weight shifting we normally do to balance a bike is greatly exaggerated.

## Old-Time Newspaper Toss

Think bicycle newspaper carriers have it easy? Roll up about ten old newspapers and fasten them with rubber bands. Ask an adult for an old bedsheet you can wreck. Cut a circular hole about two-feet wide in the middle of it. Stretch and tie the sheet between some trees or poles. Ride by the sheet from a set distance (fifteen feet is about right) and try to toss a newspaper through the hole. If you make it, you get to ride by in the opposite direction and try again. Continue until you miss. (It works out well to have friends handing you the newspapers as you ride.) You can even get a cranky neighbor to yell every time someone misses. Whoever gets the most newspapers through the hole wins.

## It's a Crash Test, Dummy

This one is just for fun, and helmets are absolutely mandatory. Go to a food or beverage store and get as many empty cardboard boxes as possible. They should be lightweight and not have hard, sharp corners. (You can flatten and soften any corners by banging them gently with a hammer or a rock. Also, tuck any loose flaps inside the boxes.) Stack up the boxes into a big tower or wall, the bigger the better. Then just take turns crashing into it and rebuilding it. It's a blast. Before you crash through the structure, just make sure there's no one behind it.

### Professor Kickstand's Cycling Advice

**Q.** Dear Professor: I live in a very, very hilly area, and I'm having trouble riding my bicycle up all the hills. Is there anything I can do?

—Billy H., Zap, ND

**A.** I always take a party pack of large balloons and a helium tank when I ride in hilly country. When I come to a hill, I just stop my bike, inflate a balloon with the helium, and tie it to my handlebars. The balloon wants to rise and helps pull me up the hill. Pedaling is much easier. If it's a very steep hill, I use several balloons. Some riders have wondered about going downhill. That's easy! Just puncture or cut the balloons loose. The weight of that helium tank will make you fly down the hill!

# The All-Day Bike Hike
## You'll Never Forget It

*"It's not the destination that's important, it's the journey."*
—Ken Kesey

**P**lanning an all-day bike hike really gives you, your family, and your buds something to look forward to. And, someday, it'll give you all something to look back on. For some reason, memories of long bike hikes never seem to fade. (Maybe it's all the oxygen going to your brain as you ride.) It can be the highlight of your summer if you plan it the right way. Here are some things to remember:

### Get Your Body Ready

Nobody can just jump on a bike for the first time and ride all day. But, in general, if you can ride for an hour without any muscle cramps or soreness, you can probably stretch it to two hours. You and your bike-hike buddies might be sore after two hours, but you'll probably make it. When the soreness goes away, try two hours again. If you still feel good after two hours, go for three hours, then four. We're not talking about hard training here—just ride like you always do. Ride around the neighborhood, see if your friends want to go for a ride. It's okay to stop and get a soda. Look at some roadkill. Throw a rock in a puddle. Take a break. Watch a cloud. In general, if you can spend half a day on your bike, just riding and goofing around, and not come home sore, you're probably ready for an all-day bike hike.

### Daylight Is Your Friend

Plan to complete the whole bike hike in "usable" daylight—that means daylight you can safely use for cycling. First check sunrise and sunset times in your newspaper, usually near the weather map. Plan to leave on your hike no earlier than a half hour after sunrise, and plan to be back no later than an hour before sunset. Usable daylight is an hour and a half less than the total amount of daylight.

## Figure Out Where to Go

A good average length for an all-day hike is eight hours of riding—four hours going somewhere and four hours coming back. Plan on going about six miles per hour. That's really not fast. Average walking speed is about four miles per hour. Six miles an hour gives you plenty of time to stop and look at weird things along the way, have snacks, and take breaks.

So where should you go? If you ride six miles per hour for four hours, you can easily go someplace about twenty-four miles away. Ask your folks to help you pick out a place. Keep the following in mind:

- It should be a place where you can get something good to eat and drink. After four hours of riding, you'll be ready for a big meal. It doesn't matter if it's fast food or a diner or a regular restaurant. Maybe it's a zoo or park with a snack bar. You don't want to carry a lot of food and drink with you (more about that later). This will be your big meal of the trip.

- It should be a place that takes you along roads that don't have much traffic or fast traffic or a lot of busy intersections. Eight hours of cars whizzing by and honking will not be enjoyable. And remember—bicycles cannot go on interstate highways. A good choice is a place that most people reach by highway that can also be reached by back roads.

- Don't get too far from civilization, at least for your first few trips. You'll probably be relying on gas-station water hoses to fill your water bottles and gas-station bathrooms for other things. And it's always nice to stop in little stores and shops that you'd just blow by if you were in a car. One of the great things about a bike hike is that you'll see and do things right in your neighborhood that few of your neighbors ever do.

- Make sure to pick a destination that will impress and entertain your friends. Hey, that's part of it. You want people to say, "You rode all the way there on a bike? Get outta here! I don't believe it." Go ahead, admit it. There's something cool about that.

### Travel the Route by Car First

This may seem like cheating, but for first-timers it's a big help. You want to know if there's any road construction or detours or narrow, busy bridges that you really don't want to cross. You or your folks may travel a road every day, but conditions may seem completely different when you're looking at them from a cyclist's point of view. You can make a map and take notes while your folks drive.

### Planning Your Grub

The plan is to buy a big lunch about four hours after you leave, so make sure you take enough money, plus some extra. While you're riding, you will get hungry. Cycling burns energy, and a good way to get steady energy is to eat a mouthful of something like nuts and raisins every half hour or so. On an eight-hour trip with a big lunch in the middle, you'll need about fourteen of these snacks. Just put fourteen teaspoons of nuts and fourteen teaspoons of raisins in a plastic sandwich bag and mix well. You're all set. If you don't like nuts and raisins, figure on half a small granola bar every half hour, so you'll need seven granola bars. Also keep in mind that every ice-cream stand along the way is going to look mighty inviting. If you

feel like stopping, do it. If you don't finish all your nuts and raisins or granola, just leave it for the squirrels. They love it. Or at least they pretend to.

## Why Be Dry?

You should figure on drinking a bicycle-type, twenty-ounce bottle of water for every hour you ride. Don't drink the whole thing all at once—a couple of good slugs every fifteen minutes or so should be good. Each person should carry one or two bottles of water and refill them at gas stations or restaurants as needed.

## Riding Duds

Be sure to wear sunscreen, but don't worry about a hat—you'll be wearing a helmet. Otherwise, wear whatever seems comfortable. Keep in mind that after you pedal for a while, you'll feel about twenty degrees warmer than someone who's just standing around. So if it's sixty degrees out, you'll feel like it's eighty. When you take a break, though, it's easy to get chilled. Having a windbreaker you can put on and take off as needed is a great idea.

Also, even in warm weather, the early morning chill can be painful on your hands stuck out there on the handlebars. You won't realize this until about fifteen minutes after you leave, and then it'll be too late to go back and get gloves. When leaving early in the morning, stick on a pair of lightweight gardening gloves or something similar for the first few miles. You won't be sorry.

Where do you keep any extra clothes when you don't have them on? That's what a rear carrier and bungees are for. It would be good to have at least one rear carrier in the group, and maybe even a file box attached, as mentioned in Chapter 14. If anybody has saddlebags, use them.

## The Night Before Your Trip

Check the weather reports and make sure you're going to have a nice day. Don't be afraid to postpone the trip if the weather is iffy. You don't want it to rain on your bike hike. Also, check your bike over for anything loose. Check your air pressure and seat height, as discussed in Chapter 13. Pack your supplies. Then go to bed. You have a big day ahead of you. . . .

## The Morning of Your Trip

Take care of as much bathroom business as you can when you get up. It's never pleasant to have a gas-station bathroom emergency along the way. Check the weather on the radio or TV and look outside. If it's foggy, wait until it's not. You need a good breakfast to get you started. Fruit and cereal is a great way to kick-start the engine that's going to power your bike all day. Check to make sure you have your water bottles, food, and money. Do you need a windbreaker or gloves? Then stretch, as discussed in Chapter 12. You'll want to do these stretches when you get where you're going, too, and then again when you get home much later. When it's at least a half hour past the official sunrise, snap on your helmet, jump on your bike, and take off!

## On the Trip

The main thing is to be safe. Remember that whenever you're riding in a group along a roadway, you need to ride single file. And you need to keep an eye on the rider in front of you in case he or she stops suddenly. Remembering to drink water often even if you're not thirsty is much more important than you think. Who wants a headache? And eating a little bit of food often will keep your energy levels up.

The *other* main thing is to have fun and experience the world around you. If you leave early in the morning, you might smell a bakery or hear a rooster or watch the sun burn through the haze. You might realize for the first time that there are foxes near your home. Or was that copper-colored blur just your imagination? You might see how much litter there is along the road and decide something must be done! Ughhh—you might smell a skunk. You might find a dollar bill floating in a puddle. You might realize how high a hill really is. You might see a pond you never saw before. You might outrun a dog. Whatever happens, you will remember it. Bike hikes are like that.

# 18 The Gold Riders
## The Bicycle in the Olympics

"Ever since I was a little boy, I've wanted to win a gold medal in the Olympics."

—Marty Nothstein, member of the U.S. Track Cycling Team, whose dream came true in the 2000 Olympics match sprint competition in Sydney, Australia

**B**ike rodeos and bike hikes and just plain riding make you stronger and more agile. You can ride longer and faster. And by reading this book, you'll probably know more than the average person about bikes and eating and drinking and stretching for cycling. But what happens when your cycling knowledge and strength and skills become WAY above average? Well, every Olympic star started somewhere. . . .

A bicycle road race was part of the first modern Olympics held in Greece in 1896—right during the world's first big bicycle craze. Exactly one hundred years later, in 1996, a newer craze, mountain biking, made its Olympic debut. In between, all kinds of track and time racing were added. Even tandem bikes were raced for a while. Now there's talk of BMX becoming an Olympic event.

At the 2000 Summer Olympics in Sydney, Australia, there were eighteen separate cycling events, the most ever. There are three main categories: road racing, mountain bike racing, and track racing.

Olympic TV coverage usually shows tiny bits of many sports, so it's hard to get the big Olympic cycling picture. Following is a snapshot of actual cycling events in the 2000 Olympic finals. Similar events are run yearly for world championships. If you see anything you like, just start practicing.

## Road Racing

Large groups of riders race together on a course of regular roads and streets. In 2000, in separate competitions, 154 men raced about 143 miles, and 57 women raced about 77 miles.

## Road Race Individual Time Trials

Riders on road bikes start one by one and race the clock for the fastest time. In 2000, the course was just over nine miles long, through city and suburban streets and roads. Thirty-nine men raced for three laps or about twenty-eight miles. Winning time: fifty-seven minutes, forty seconds. Twenty-four women raced for two laps or about nineteen miles. Winning time: forty-two minutes.

## Mountain Bike Racing (also called Cross-Country)

Large groups of riders race together over obstacles, forest roads, fields, and dirt and gravel paths in a large park. In 2000, forty-nine men and thirty women raced in separate competitions.

*Gold in Them Thar Hills*
*Men's and Women's Mountain Bike Cross-Country became an Olympic event in 1996.*

## Track Bike Racing

This is the busiest Olympic cycling category. Events are held indoors on a steeply banked oval track called a velodrome (VEL-uh-drome). In the Olympics, the track is 250 meters around. Because the track is banked, the bicycles handle as if they are going in a straight line—very little steering is required. Track bicycles are extremely light and built for aerodynamics. They have no brakes, and the pedals move all the time—they can't coast. To slow the bike, the rider simply slows up on the pedals. Here are the Olympic track cycling events as of 2000:

Q: Why can't bicycles stand up on their own?
A: Because they're two-tired.

- **Time Trials**
These are quick, frantic races in which each rider races as fast as he or she can against the clock. It's considered the most exhausting cycling event. In the 2000 finals, sixteen men raced one kilometer (four laps). Winning time: 1 minute, 1.6 seconds. Seventeen women raced five hundred meters (two laps). Winning time: 34.14 seconds.

**My Bike's Smaller Than Your Bike**

An Australian man named Neville Pattern built the world's smallest rideable bicycle in 1988. Now get out your ruler. The wheels were just over three-quarters of an inch across. He rode it for almost thirteen feet.

- **Individual Sprint (also called Match Sprint)**
After a series of elimination rounds, two riders finally fight it out for the gold in a best-of-three competition. Each race is three laps. The riders may go slowly for two laps, studying each other's moves, then blast off in the last lap up to fifty miles per hour to the finish. There are separate competitions for men and women.

- **Individual Pursuit**
Two riders start at opposite sides of the track and try to pass each other. If neither passes the other, the best time wins. The final race for the gold comes after a series of qualifying rounds. Olympic men race four kilo-

meters (sixteen laps) in about four minutes. Women race three kilometers (twelve laps) in about three minutes.

## • Team Pursuit

This men's event is similar to the Individual Pursuit, but with two teams of four riders each. They start on opposite sides of the track and race for four kilometers (sixteen laps). Riders take turns leading their teams around the track, trying to catch the other team. For a team to win, its third member must catch up to the third member of the other team. If no team catches the other, the race is won when the third member of the fastest team crosses the finish line.

## • Points Race

This is one of the most action-packed and unpredictable Olympic track cycling events. In the 2000 Olympics, seventeen women raced twenty-four kilometers (98 laps) and eleven men raced forty kilometers (160 laps). Points are scored by being ahead of the pack at certain times (every fifth or sixth lap). There's a lot of sprinting. If a rider can break away and go ahead of the pack by a full lap—and stay ahead for the rest of the race—it's possible to win even without the most points. But there's another twist—the winner of the last lap gets his or her points doubled. It's not over till it's over.

## • The Madison

This men's race is named after the old Madison Square Garden arena in New York, which was famous for bicycle racing in the early 1900s. It runs sixty kilometers (240 laps) for the Olympics, and uses two-man teams. As in the Points Race, riders try to win points by sprinting ahead of the pack every five to six laps. During the race, team members must switch off, as in a relay. The team member being replaced grabs his partner's hand and slings him and his bike along for extra speed.

- **Olympic Sprint**

This is a quick three-lap race. Like the Team Pursuit, the Olympic Sprint starts with two teams on opposite sides of the track. The teams have three members. Each member must lead his team for one lap, then drop out. The third riders for each time then finish the race alone in a mad dash.

- **Keirin**

Pronounced KAY-rin, this two-kilometer (eight-lap) men's event originated in Japan, where it is a popular spectator sport. In the 2000 final, six racers pedaled behind a motorcycle for six laps. The motorcycle sets the pace and gradually speeds up to about thirty miles per hour. Then it pulls off the track, and the racers sprint a wild two laps to the finish.

# 19 There's a Lot More Fun Out There

## More Extremely Cool Bike Events

*"If it was easy, then everyone would do it."*

—Lon Haldeman, former winner and now director of the Race Across America

There may be gold and prestige and TV coverage in the Olympics, but there are plenty of other opportunities for competition and fun in the bicycle world.

### The Triathlon

Do you like to swim, cycle, and run? Try the triathlon (try-ATH-lon). This grueling event typically combines swimming for about a mile, a 25-mile bicycle time trial, and a 6-mile run, all on the same day, with as few breaks as possible! Think that's rough? The most famous triathlon, the Hawaii Ironman, features a 2.4-mile swim, a 112-mile bicycle time trial, and a 26-mile running marathon—all completed within seventeen hours! It was started by a U.S. Navy commander in 1978, and versions are now held under the "Ironman" name all over the world. The triathlon became an Olympic event for men and women in 2000, but it's not considered a cycling event. Apparently there's too much running and swimming going on. . . .

### The Race Across America

Want to do some quick sightseeing? Try the world's longest nonstop bicycle race— the Race Across America (RAAM). About twenty-five racers compete on a route

# The Cycling Life
## It Never Ends

> "The bicycle courier is a direct descendant of the cowboys and the gauchos. All deliveries exist to be performed in a fluid motion of grace."
>
> —Brooks, from "500 West Madison," on www.bikereader.com

Love for cycling often begins under a Christmas tree or on a birthday when you get your first set of wheels. Even if it's a hand-me-down, your bike gives you freedom, fun, exercise, and a chance to explore and win races, get places, and even learn how mechanical things work. There's a lot to love. A bike can even lead to a hobby or a job that gives you a special place in the world. There are top scientists out there who say their early experience with bicycles helped them become interested in inventing things. And there are top athletes out there, famous throughout the world, who started on the road to success the day they first learned to ride.

There's lots you can do on a bike, now and throughout your whole life. Meet some people who have cycling in their hearts.

## A "Couple" of Bike Nuts

If you love cycling, it's great to be a schoolteacher—you have all summer to ride! Jim Grill grew up in rural New Jersey, where biking was the way to get around. It was perfectly normal for him to ride forty miles to the beach and thirty miles to the college where he studied to be a teacher. Guess what? Jim got very good at cycling. He became a racer and coach and a phys ed teacher. At the beach he met a girl named Paula, who was also learning to be a teacher. For their first date, Jim took Paula to watch the Olympic cycling trials in New York. She soon became a bike nut as well, and the two got married. When they weren't teaching in the local schools, they were at cycling events—Jim as a racer and coach, and Paula as a race judge. They got better and better at what they did, and soon Jim was spending the summers as a cycling coach at the Olympic Training Center in Colorado. There he trained Greg LeMond, who later became the first American to win the Tour de France. Meanwhile, Paula rose to the top of the cycling world as highest-ranking judge in international cycling, even judging the Olympics. Then, every September, Jim and Paula Grill would return to their local schools and become regular teachers again. When your teachers ask you what you did all summer, ever wonder what *they* did?

## Here's Your Package! See Ya!

In a city, when a package has to get quickly from one office building to another, it's often quickest to send it by bicycle messenger. Bikes can zip by traffic jams, and parking is never a problem. Being a bike messenger is one way for a bike lover to make money. Bike messengers usually work about eight or ten hours a day, carrying envelopes and packages in a bag slung low across their backs. They get addresses and orders by cell phone or pager and easily ride seventy-five miles a day, making as many as sixty deliveries in all kinds of weather. They get paid by the delivery, so they try to be as fast as they can, figuring out strategies to beat the traffic, find shortcuts, and combine trips. They become very strong riders with quick reflexes and funky nicknames. Frankie Baby, a bike messenger in New York City, said all the speed and the dodging of cars make him feel as if he's in a video game. Handlebars = joysticks?

## Justin Case You're Talented

He takes his bicycle apart as he rides it, rearranging all the parts. The front wheel becomes his steering wheel, and the pedals go where his seat was. All the while he keeps riding around the circus ring, and piece by piece he puts the bike back together again. Ta-da! The crowd goes wild. Like Bart Simpson with a fake French accent, he teases them, "What, you never saw a bicycle repairman?" Next he rides a six-inch-high bicycle through a flaming hoop. The crowd screams for more. He shrugs, and from a shoe box pulls out a four-inch-high bicycle. He gives them more. He's Justin Case, a trick cyclist in shows like the Big Apple Circus. Though he studied art in his home country of Australia, he always felt as comfortable on two wheels as most people feel on two feet. He remembers when he was four, wondering why his twelve-year-old brother couldn't ride as well as he: "It's not that difficult!" I remember thinking. "What's the problem?" Today Justin (who won't reveal his real name) travels the world entertaining people on his bicycles. And when he's not entertaining others with his wheels, he entertains himself. For fun he goes mountain biking.

## Starting Young

Ashley Kimmet of Pennsylvania started splashing toward cycling championships in 1983 when she was just three months old. She began a "Swim with Mommy" program in a local pool, and for the next fourteen years, swimming was her sport. Results? Strong lungs and heart, and long, smooth muscles that just don't quit. By high school, she could run faster and longer than most kids and earned a spot on the track-and-field team. About this time she discovered cycling. The Lehigh Valley Velodrome was close by, and she enjoyed a few years of racing around its banked track. Once again, she turned out to be faster than most kids. Results? A second-place finish in the Junior Cycling World Championships and an opportunity to represent the United States at the Goodwill Games. Now she has her eye on the Olympics, where she'll be young enough to compete in women's cycling through at least 2012. "Women racers seem to hit their peak in their late twenties, early thirties, so I have a long way to go," she said. She sure does. Many of her

## Professor Kickstand's Cycling Advice

**Q.** Dear Professor: My bike is kind of slow, and I've heard there are oils or sprays that can make it faster. Can you make any recommendations?—Pete S., Cut Shin, KY

**A.** Dear Pete: The next time your folks are cooking a rump roast, ask them to save the fat drippings for you in an old tin can. When the drippings have cooled, coat your bike with the rump-roast grease. And let it sit in the hot sun until it smells mighty meaty. Then get on the bike and ride until you find a roaming pack of large, hungry dogs. The dogs will get one whiff, think you're a giant traveling rump roast, and become very enthusiastic. In scientific testing, this method has increased the speed of the average bicycle by 21 percent.

training rides are ninety miles long.

## Pedaling Police

In sunny Fort Lauderdale, Florida, the police patrols by bicycle all year long and officer Dominic Angiolillo couldn't be happier. He says it lets him combine one of his favorite pastimes with his job and gives him tons of exercise as he rides about thirty miles per day on patrol. Officer Angiolillo is one of about twenty thousand "cops on bikes" in the U.S. Bikes let police officers  sneak up on troublemakers, jump off, and instantly deal with a problem, whether it's a pickpocket, a drug dealer, or a prowler. Mountain bikes can go places cars can't, faster than a trouble-maker can run. Bike-riding police officers go to school to learn tricks like the "power slide"—passing a fleeing suspect, then turning around instantly in a skid. Yikes! Face-to-face with the law! The suspect is often so surprised, he or she gives up on the spot.

# The Bike That Flew to France

It had two tiny wheels, pedals, and a 137-pound professional cyclist in the saddle, and on June 12, 1979, it flew across twenty-three miles of open water from England to France. It was the Gossamer Albatross—part bicycle, part hang glider, and the winner of the $200,000 Kremer Prize for the first human-powered vehicle to fly across the English Channel.

Named after an extremely light fabric and the world's largest seabird, the Gossamer Albatross weighed only about seventy pounds but had a wingspan of ninety-six feet. Its framework was made mostly of carbon tubes covered in plastic sheeting. The power for the propeller was provided by a pilot pushing regular bicycle pedals. To get across the Channel, Bryan Allen from California had to pedal for two hours and forty-nine minutes, often only inches above the waves. Wilbur and Orville would have been proud.

# The Biggest, Tallest, Smallest, Longest, and Kookiest

### In Case You Can't Figure Out 27 Speeds

Leon Chassman of Michigan added gears from old bikes until he came up with a bike that had 1,500 gear combinations—a world record.

### Get a Ladder and Climb Aboard

The biggest rideable bicycle in the world is called the Frankencycle. It was first ridden by Steve Gordon of California in 1989. The wheels are 10 feet in diameter, and the whole bike is 11 feet, 2 inches tall.

### A Really Looooong Ride

It traveled only 368 feet, but it was 84 feet, 11 inches long and held 40 riders. In 1998, it took the record for the longest two-wheel bicycle ever built.

### Watch Out for Planes

The tallest rideable unicycle was 101 feet, 9 inches high—about the height of a ten-story building. A rider pedaled it 376 feet in Las Vegas in October 1980. And yes, there was a safety wire in case he fell.

### Not for Your Baby Brother

Sixteen students at a community college in Michigan built the world's largest tricycle in 1998. The front wheel was over 15 feet in diameter, the back wheels were over 7 feet, and the whole thing towered 23 feet, 4 inches above the road.

### Watch Out for Insects, Too!

The smallest rideable unicycle is 8 inches high with a wheel diameter of 7/10 of an inch. Its longest trip was 24 feet, 10 ¼ inches when it was ridden on the Guinness World Records television show in 1999.

### They Must Really Love Each Other

A husband and wife in France ride the world's smallest tandem bicycle—14 inches long.

# Your Bicycle: Get to Know It!

Though we show a mountain bike here—currently the most popular two-wheel vehicle—most bikes include some or all of these parts:

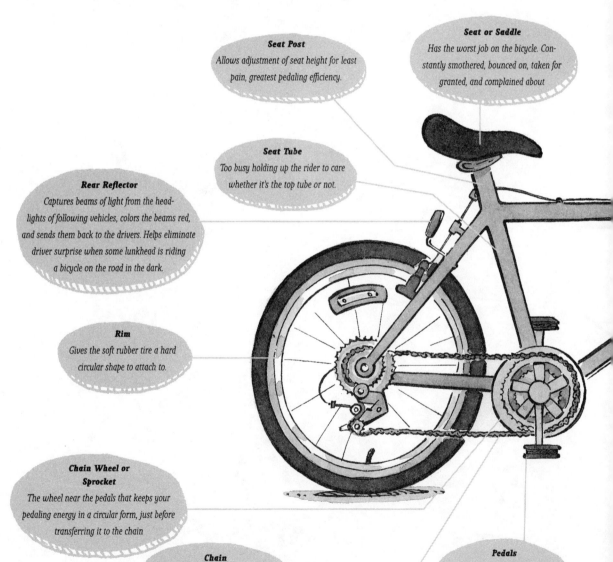

**Seat Post**
Allows adjustment of seat height for least pain, greatest pedaling efficiency.

**Seat or Saddle**
Has the worst job on the bicycle. Constantly smothered, bounced on, taken for granted, and complained about

**Seat Tube**
Too busy holding up the rider to care whether it's the top tube or not.

**Rear Reflector**
Captures beams of light from the headlights of following vehicles, colors the beams red, and sends them back to the drivers. Helps eliminate driver surprise when some lunkhead is riding a bicycle on the road in the dark.

**Rim**
Gives the soft rubber tire a hard circular shape to attach to.

**Chain Wheel or Sprocket**
The wheel near the pedals that keeps your pedaling energy in a circular form, just before transferring it to the chain

**Chain**
Takes your energy from pedaling and transfers it to the rear wheel.

**Pedals**
Two little footpads where the engine attaches to the bicycle. Yes, the engine—YOU!

**Shift Levers**

Usually two twist grips or click levers. These let you decide how many times you want the back wheel to go around each time you pedal.

**Handlebars**

A bike's "steering wheel." Also provides a place to rest hands when finished riding "no hands."

**Top Tube**

The #1 most popular tube on the bicycle

**Brake Levers**

One slows down or stops the front wheel; the other slows down or stops the back wheel. Handy when speeding toward rim of Grand Canyon.

**Front Reflector**

Captures beams of light from the headlights of oncoming vehicles and sends them back to the drivers. Helps eliminate driver surprise when some lunkhead is riding a bicycle on the road in the dark.

**Front Fork and Hub**

A place for the front wheel to attach to the bicycle.

**Spokes**

Thin metal wires that provide a lightweight way to attach the rim to the hub. They are also highly effective in thwapping baseball cards and creating a satisfying thum, thum, thum noise.

**Down Tube**

A tube that's feeling kind of sad because it's not the top tube.

**Tire**

An air-filled rubber circle that puts a layer of air between the rider and the road. Smooths out your ride.

# Select Bibliography

Ballantine, Richard, and Richard Grant. *Ultimate Bicycle Book*. New York: DK Publishing, 1998.

Ditchfield, Christin. *Cycling*. New York: Children's Press, 2000.

Garvy, Helen. *How to Fix Your Bicycle*. Santa Cruz, Calif.: Shire Press, 1980.

George, Barbara. *Bicycle Road Racing*. Minneapolis, Minn.: Lerner Publications Company, 1977.

———. *Bicycle Track Racing*. Minneapolis, Minn.: Lerner Publications Company, 1977.

Hall, David. *Discover the Wonder*. Glenview, Ill.: Scott Foresman and Company, 1994.

Leek, Stephen, and Sybil Leek. *The Bicycle—That Curious Invention*. Nashville, Tenn./New York: Thomas Nelson, Inc., 1973.

Loeper, John J. *Away We Go: On Bicycles in 1898*. Saddle Brook, N.J.: American Book Stratford Press, 1982.

Lyttle, Richard B. *The Complete Beginner's Guide to Bicycling*. Garden City, N.Y.: Doubleday and Company, 1974.

McPhee Gribble Publishers. *Bicycles: All About Them*. New York: Puffin, 1976.

Murphy, Jim. *Two Hundred Years of Bicycles*. New York: J. B. Lippincott, 1983.

Sullivan, George. *Better Bicycling for Boys and Girls*. New York: Dodd, Mead & Company, 1984.

# Index